Persuasions of Fall

Persuasions of Fall

Ann Lauinger

THE UNIVERSITY OF UTAH PRESS

Salt Lake City

The Agha Shahid Ali Prize in Poetry
Series Edited by Katharine Coles

09 08 07 06 05 04
5 4 3 2 1

The Defiance House Man colophon is a registered trademark of
the University of Utah Press. It is based upon a four-foot-tall,
Ancient Puebloan pictograph (late PIII) near Glen Canyon, Utah.

LIBRARY OF CONGRESS CATALOGING-IN-PUBLICATION DATA

Lauinger, Ann 1948–
  Persuasions of fall / Ann Lauinger.
    p. cm.
  ISBN 0-87480-797-2 (pbk. : alk. paper)
  I. Title
  PS3612.A944P47 2004
  811'.6—dc22

                        2003022548

For Joe with love

Take my heart that hollers . . .

CONTENTS

PART ONE

THE COMPANY OF FOOLS

Praise the small boom of frogs
      in spring woods
for complicating green: leaf buds,
the warbler's breast, the glassy pond,
      amphibious slime.

Praise the deadpan mimicry
      of absent masters,
antic dance on laundry-line
where shirts and socks relieved of bodies
      swell and flutter.

Praise the broken eggs and praise
      whoever dropped them.
Smooth virtue deserves a smash—
and what pleasure's more reliable
      than a decent omelet?

Praise the empty fist that buys
      safe passage
through the evil wood: no maps, no money.
It's hard, learning to trust the imp
      in improvident.

Praise surprise, that benign bomber
      manically bent
on blowing us sky-wide. Praise
his crafty sidekick, picklock laughter.
      Praise the company of fools.

FALLINGWATER

Dear Kaufmann,

        Are you a brave man?
I'm back from Bear Run, yes, but *the visit*
to the waterfall in the woods stays with me.

The view is, you have said, your chief concern.
Of course. The panorama is sublime.
In spring, the falls spit foam in the sun's eye;
they throw off diamonds, milk, opaline fire
before they drop away.
Winter sculpts the water's frozen fall,
a black marble mirror . . .

And so forth. Views are exhilarating,
especially when they're fortified in stone.
Anyone can heap together a tower,
Kaufmann, or live in one. I don't advise it:
stone eminence breeds a basilisk gaze.
To live with things, you have to listen to them.

At Bear Run I listened. How shall I tell
you what I heard? A poet might call it music,
if one sole note repeated makes a tune.
At first the monotony of water splashing
half-hypnotized me. Limp as a mesmerist's geek,
I listened and despaired. From this onrush,
unceasing, undifferentiated,
what Form could ever struggle into being?
I went on listening, until the Sameness lifted,
as the heavy gold curtain at the opera
scrolls slowly upward after the overture.

It came at the end, beside the stream, to chaos,
the brutal cry of beautiful un-making.
Each staccato instant, change hammered change—
as in the falling water, so in the furious
currents occulted beneath my traitor skin.

The house I want to build asks daring—
not of me, Kaufmann, but of you.
I shall cantilever concrete slabs
over falls and stream, layered like birthday cake.
My job's a conjuror's trick, mere cunning.
The question, Kaufmann, is: have you the courage
not simply to look at the waterfalls, but to live with them?

Yours most sincerely,

F. Lloyd Wright

In 1936 Frank Lloyd Wright built the Edgar J. Kaufmann house, Fallingwater,
on Bear Run in Fayette County, Pennsylvania. Italicized phrases are quoted from
Wright's correspondence.

PET FISH

The kindness of children has
a mortal touch. They are Noahs
in negative, who summon fish
in pairs to an ark that encloses

a docile flood: figurines,
one pale, spindly plant,
gravel, pink and green.
We call it an experiment.

In the beginning were Anonni and Anonna,
most carefully carried from Woolworth's
like a take-out order of wonton in a
wire-handled cardboard purse

and most lovingly overfed
till they choked in dirty water,
and fresh generations were led
in innocence home to slaughter.

Who'd ever guess there would be
so many ways fish could die?
Their silence had subtexts, but we
wouldn't voice them. We let silence lie.

Some curled like potato chips,
their scales invaded by rot;
in that contorting grip
suppleness turned spasmodic.

Some slipped to the garish tank floor,
composed (while decomposing)
as if to help us ignore
something tactless, as if apologizing.

We expect too much of fish.
In cartoons, they play all the fat
parts, act wise and waggish,
inevitably humiliate the cat.

Once we thought life would triumph:
a pineapple, plump as her name
and ripening, produced a bumper
crop of babies. She ate

the lot. Then she died too—
naturally—of overfeeding.
But now, as if life were cartoon
and merely seeing, believing,

down the porcelain slope she speeds
flickering under our eyes
with the dazzle of ice-skate blades,
as the children squeal, "She's alive!"

Comets and fancy goldfish,
guppies and tri-colored sharks,
zebra fish, mollies, pipe fish,
swordtails and neon tetras:

I ask you all to forgive us.
Lessons in the hard things—hope,
responsibility, love, loss—
cost so much. And fish are cheap.

FEBRUARY ELEGY FOR AL

in memory of Al Sadler

Weather no one manages: February,
bastard month, the season of amputations.
All things raw, misshapen or graceless, ill-willed
                              thrive in this climate.

No mistake about it: a blue-eyed malice
flicked you down, to make something ugly happen.
You, whose wit swam most (like the eider-duck) at
                              ease in the big swells.

You refused to cherish the cloudy secrets
power hugs, your outermost house plain air. You
heard at every turn in the maze of creatures
                              more than their music.

Morning. Foot to foot lie the snow-laced hills, the
river's black glass twinning the western shore-line.
Currents, churn; and seagulls, come scatter stillness:
                              symmetry chokes me.

Afternoon. The temperature drops. Encroaching
ice obliges me—only now I mourn the
damage. Change and changelessness never fooled you,
                              agile in all winds.

Evening. Ice floes shackle the iron river.
What comes after? You knew to keep inventing.
Ice unfolds in flame, and a cardinal fire
                              fuels the darkness.

GOOD NIGHT, SLEEP TIGHT

Fingers curled on nothing, little Caliban
sleeps secure, already dreaming how
much of the world will come away in his fists.
As in the womb, distinctions between man
and fish are moot. This island's his; he rests
in shallows. Glassy gaze and bobbling head
have rocked him to safe haven, where the bough
may break, but tumbles someone else from bed.

Now Sycorax, who used to raise and quell
a hurricane for fun, can't sleep at night.
Elion asheroth baroch . . . no spell
can keep him hers, when simple *lullabye*
plummets him fathoms. Where? The stars won't tell,
and let the sunrise drown their figured light.

IRONING

for Honey

There ought to be a better name for it: *time*
for such a power has too puny a ring.
In a narrow kitchen smelling of warm cotton
and hot metal (it was a tight squeeze
slipping past the shiny tethered iron)
I measured the length and breadth of paradise.

It's lost now, like any respectable paradise,
or stolen. Either way the culprit is time—
four-letter word for turning into iron
a honeyed kiss or a gilded ring.
If we'd noticed time in the kitchen, a squeeze
could have squelched him then; thin as old cotton

drawers he was, and worn. But we didn't cotton
on to his tricks, too busy in paradise.
It was so full there, nothing more could squeeze
inside—no room—but we had plenty of time.
And on my finger twirled the magic ring
that spins a safety more absolute than iron.

We croon, and quiet clicking from the iron
counterpoints gospel tunes wispy as cotton.
I puzzle over the chariots and the ring
of angels swooping to carry us off to Paradise,
which I can see is right here all this time.
Or could there be another one? I squeeze

my eyelids very tight because when you squeeze,
it dazzles. No need. Here the radiant iron,
a tiny hearth from once upon a time,
organizes all: smooth and scented cotton
dangles overhead; the boughs of paradise
bear silken colors like an opal ring.

Nothing happened. No catastrophic ring
shrilled at the door. But something came to squeeze
me right out of our narrow paradise.
I look back at the laundry ready to iron,
a basket full of damp, crumpled cotton—
rags all, and all for the pockets of time.

Pack away your precious ring in cotton,
relic of your faded time in paradise.
It will squeeze your heart; draw tears of iron.

THE AENEAS VARIATIONS

for Joe

1.

In the early light, neck bowed, he works at translation.
Alone at his desk, he concentrates, identifies,
summons scattered fragments to their rightful places.
The charts he loves are pinned on the walls. Their calibrated
depths, concentric pools of blue, reflect like mirrors
what he knows. Trouble is, he's sailing somewhere else.
Can these austere enchantments reinvent him?

2.

After embracing the air, after the groaning prophetess,
after the funeral pyres quenched with milk and wine,
he threads the clamorous ways—Grand Marshal in a parade
of two—tossing sops and waving the branch of gold.
Its dangling leaves tinkle absurdly (like her earrings)
whenever silence fractures the din. Obliterate
the past. He stalks her through the weightless mob. His task
henceforth is to remember the future. Scented oil
and sweat prick his eyes to tears. Tearing his curls
by fistfuls he shouts, "All flesh is freakish! Forgive, forgive!"
She who has kept her back to him, head bent low
now turns. Unmollified and mute as stone, she shows
her mole's face, shiny skin over empty sockets.

3.

He keeps forgetting his pockets are full of shivered glass
and lifts the bloodied fingers to his mouth. The work
of reassembly beckons. He should have understood
that tears are not in things. Not in the brown teapot
with its mended lid, not in the lamplight soft on drawn
shades, or the carved menageries of tall facades:
in no hue or form that earth or sky confers.
Tears are in the words for things. His neck, his voice
inflect an ancient burden: plural, conditional, imperfect.

WITHOUT YOU

All night I dreamed I was fixing the flat tires
on my 16-wheeler with a salad fork.
The night before, I was on the roof in snow-
shoes. Where will it end? Without you I'm like a
fish struggling into a pair of pantyhose.

Without you, the kitchen sink gets all choked up,
the hot water runs cold, the toilet just runs,
and I can't screw the lightbulb in straight even
when it really wants to change. Tomorrow I
must buy a shower curtain for the birdbath.

Come home! The cats are witless with grief. Ginger
and Freud drool on your pillow, and Dim Sum chews
my toes. (Do you think that could be affecting
my dreams?) You know how you badgered me to change
the sheets? It's done! The stripes go the other way!

If you won't come back, at least send a postcard
and clippings—hair or nails. I track you with pins
on the wall map and I spin yarn from your hair.
Whistle, darling: I'll be there. Love gives me wings
and a kayak. All I need is your address.

TWO ONION ÉTUDES

1. Andante

Think
about an onion
and you return to the
onion: flesh on flesh on flesh...
An onion is not like other things.
Other things are like the onion
for which no simile can serve,
ground of similitude
itself.

2. Adagio

April dusk, butcher block, garlic
        from the small mud-colored jar, onion
out of the heavy black-glazed urn, a widow's womb.
                I chop and crush.

        Light dies, the catbird's rasp falls into silence.
Only the pulped flesh cries wisdom
        (my fingertips and tongue burn with it)
                black dirt.

KNIVES

We lay dangerous things out between us.
The knives are washed and dried and shining

dark on the white counter; no ambush
lurks in the drawers. Their carbon steel

looks to me mottled with violence
they might do: the slip-grip sliced thumb

or barefoot amputation. I've never mastered
the Julia Child technique, can't let the broad

blade fall of its own weight. When you
chop, the edge strikes the board at just

the right angle, making short soundless
work of onions doomed to the pot.

Each blade you sweep down
the whetstone sings a high thin tune.

I instinctively choose the wrong knife
for the job: serrated for peeling,

a paring knife to dice with. When I
sharpen, I take the edge right off.

It's a kitchen tango, darling,
cooks' paso doble of risky glitter,

a knife's edge perfected
by daily diminution.

SNAKESKIN

Snagged on the branch
of a failing rosebush:
a cloudy bleached-brown
cellophane tube.

I said:

I'm not the type
to search for signs.
But look at this
tattered bunting
flapping over occupied territory.

You said:

I don't believe
in signs.

I said:

Snakes in my garden!

You said:

It's a long tradition.

I said:

Where? How many?
They're fleshy and cold.
What'll I do when I weed?

You said:

Ambush confirms
the hidden life.

I said:

Once in a French village
I turned a corner:
entrails coiled in
a butcher's window,
hearts with their slimy flaps
were propped on casual display.

You said:

Look. This skin
and its occupant
parted on equal terms,
the one vanished,
the other nearly
invisible.

I said:

Vanished where? And
not invisible, not yet.

You said:

Into its life. Ok,
translucent.

I said:

A ragged
flag of truce?
I think it's a sign.

You said:

Aren't there terrors
and pleasures
enough
in plain view?

THE POEM HE WILL NOT WRITE

> Hence, viper thoughts, that coil around my mind,
>   Reality's dark dream!
> I turn from you and listen to the wind . . .
>   Coleridge, "Dejection: An Ode"

At his desk, where Sara thinks he is writing,
he is, in fact, engaged in examining his pockets,
arranging their contents in a semi-circle
        compass jack-knife comb
        laudanum vial (empty)
        bit of blue wax
        acorn

I may not hope from outward forms to win
The passion and the life, whose fountains are within.
    Well, he pays dear for his presumption:
a post-box stuffed with letters to himself,
    the bony grip tightening on his throat.

He mends some pens, checks his supply of paper,
    but what is this noise . . .
A mounting roar, as raving breakers beat
The sea to foam, and hiss in petulant retreat . . .
    No. He will rewrite that. He is miles inland.

The noise insists, draws him from his desk.
    Outside, a hard, tail-thumping wind
shoves him back and bangs the door.

Saplings, sacred acrobats, sweep
    the cliff wall; the path to the garden
        makes a dizzy mosaic of shivered
            sun and shade, Heraclitus' river.
        Vines and branches, self-scourgers,

strain to unseam themselves;
a gypsy glitter trembles in the undersides of leaves.

He opens his mouth to proclaim
        the approach of angels
        the life in motion, within him and abroad,
        or maybe just to call Sara

but the hurling wind empties his voice.

LONDON BRIDGE

London Bridge is falling down.
Children shout what we won't say:
silence is shapelier than sound,

the voice of ruins more profound
than any tune steel cables play
until the bridge is falling down.

Then let it fall. Stones on the ground,
a scattered music, can't betray
the silence shapelier than sound;

impartially the din will drown
arpeggios with the ass's bray
when bridge and all come falling down.

Ship's keel, satin heel, common noun—
the truest builders but grope their way
toward silence, shapelier than sound,

that perfect, that entropic round
beyond the cast of breath or clay.
London Bridge is falling down.
Silence is shapely. Make no sound.

FABLE

Look to the burrowing fieldmouse,
swallow threading the air:
the hawk's shadow may fall suddenly
yet comes as no surprise.
It's the pure intent of animals
that makes them seem wise.

Therefore relentless intellect prowls
the halls in fury or despair
till sightless busts in symmetry
converge. Are we God's spies?
A glimpse of the sickle moon stops hearts.
Urgent. Please advise.

So here you are on the dolphin's back:
salt spray and glare,
plunging sea and land compose
harmonies. If you're wise,
you know you're lucky. Back on shore
you'll have a knack for lies.

LULLABYE

Put judgment to sleep,
put baby to bed.
Loosen the fists,
lay down the head.

Eyes be lidded;
sight is stark
and flint enough
to burn down the dark.

Rock softly, cradle,
till thoughts be dumb,
deaf to emphasis.
Silence, come,

and fumbling dreamer,
foot bravely your part:
ghost fandango
to the squeezebox heart.

THE WIG

I hated that styrofoam skull, your faceless, white
alter ego: my Mom, the coffee cup.
What's bald as an egg by day and thatched by night?
My private sphinx. I thought I would throw up.
You mocked your benighted, *shaytl*ed mother-in-law,
yet dropped that rat's nest on your close-cropped head
with the satisfied air of someone settling a score.
It frightened me, this making bits of you dead.
I wanted to shake you: nature is not scorned
(that much my twelve-year-old body had guessed),
and wigs are for chemo. But you would not be warned.
You longed to enlist with the ravaged, lose a breast;
till then, you practiced piecemeal suicide.
This was war. Where could a daughter hide?

ADAM THINKS

Somewhere else, the glass-green wall
of ocean towers and breaks. Leviathan
and all the little fishes swim where they will,
glide through deeps, flunder and smack at the sun.

≈

Here in verb-less Paradise
Adam feels useless.
In the face of thwart growths
of bloom and root, brush
and vine in knotted wefts,
in the face of so much *is*,
he lays down his tools,
he breathes out spirit,
sinks back into clay.

≈

Next morning (and there is a next morning)
Adam blinks in the warmth,
pets the companionable voles curled at his side.
Disentangling the titmouse who roosts in his hair,
he yawns, not upright yet, and sees—oh, lightness
stepping through the glade, catching at wayward
shoots that glance in the green unsettled wake
of its soft advancing—what angel without wings?
His hands interrogate the thunk-thunk in his chest.
What should he say?
Bone of my bones, flesh of my flesh,
he crows, joyful.
And thinks: *It will all be different now.*

ADAM DIGS

When Adam delved and Eve span,
Who was then the gentleman?

Adam digs

Eve says

Butterflies dawdling above furze

Adam digs

Eve says

At dawn grackles rise flockmeal
Luminant spattering stars

Adam prunes

Eve says

Moss-stepped catamount
Darkling amaranth and ginger
Flensing hawk-shrill

Adam ties back vines

Eve says

Delicate glitter of ophidian imbrication

The serpent cocks its crested head

Adam digs

WILD MUSHROOMS

Never mind getting to know our names:
Slippery Jill, Green Stain, Stinky Squid,
Inky Cap, Angel's Wings, Devil's Urn.
What you need to know is anonymous.
We are earth's organs, her oracles.
Ask what you will, there's only one answer:
self is a fraud—flim-flam phoenix,
articulate toy, a tease to distract
for a time—no ticket to eternity.
All marvels, mechanisms, mastery—
mere matter. All suffer their metamorphoses.
What do you want with wildflowers?
Let the sun, senile and oversexed,
lavish his light on their lying designs.
Turn aside, step to the sunless
margins of the path. With moss and mold
we hold dank dominion here. On dung
and leaf-litter, living and lifeless wood,
our flesh unfolds. Here is your fellowship:
sacs and caps and cups and cortex
fringed coral fingers and fat thumbs
sponge of bone-marrow, birthmarks, blotches
bright cinnabar beads of blood.

SPARES

My mother used to beg the dentist to pull
every damn tooth in her head and spare her the grief.
Typically, she preferred the grand gesture (annul
nature!) and scorned small measures (brushing her teeth).
She sailed to sleep by way of Candy Land;
M&Ms, peanut brittle, chocolate kisses,
Demerol, and Librium freighted the nightstand.
At last my bionic mother got her wishes:
capped teeth and a stomach tube. Her days afloat
in the lounger were buoyed by thrillers and soda pop
(later diapers, a catheter, air through a hole in the throat).
"I don't have to bother eating"; she waved at the glop
being piped to her guts. As if she'd cheated fate,
she flashed me a joyful grin. Her teeth looked great.

ENOUGH

I get a kick out of these poets
who are always discovering *it is enough*.
Rain tattooing the windows *is enough*.
Your warm flesh beaded with damp *is enough*.
Enough is the stern mesa, the spawning ocean,
this hammer, that sparrow, our sagging porch steps—
enough with *enough*!

Ladies & gentlemen, a question:
Why this restless stringing and restringing words
if *it is enough*?
And why is my heart like a short-legged dog
that jumps and jumps
for a piece of meat on the table?

KYUSHU ECLOGUE

Scene: Kyushu. A small garden pavilion

Time: Early evening, late May, the year 901

Speakers: Two Heian poets, Sugawara Michizane (845–903)
and Lady Ise (?877–?940)

M: Affinities, Lady Ise, correspondences:
Blue leaps to blue. This iris is a flame.

I: Consider their origins, Michizane:
Fire from fuel, flowers from seed.

M: Consider that the same turf
Feeds flame and bloom.

I: Eiko's kiss was petaled, Keiko's touch burned.
So you told me.

M: My soup was hot, my soup grew cold:
Same soup.

I: You ate up the beans but left the radishes
Untouched.

M: And if tomorrow I eat the radishes
But leave the beans . . . ?

I: Tomorrow there may be none.
Everything longs for rain.

M: Rain falls, ceases, falls.
Longing endures.

I: I know where rain furrows rice-powder
And no peonies bloom.

M: There, one sows comfort
   And cultivates distress.

I: My friend, not every soil
   Will bear all crops.

M: When frogs jump in a pond,
   All make the same splash.

I: Listen: each frog croaks
   Its own note.

M: The plucked string sounds many notes
   But remains the same.

I: How different the same note sounds
   In June or December.

M: Yet June brings round December,
   December June.

I: Still, you sweat and crave snow,
   Shiver and dream of roses.

M: Metaphors, Lady Ise,
   And all for the same desire.

I: Why then, Michizane, do you not
   Lay down your brush?

M: A thousand jackdaws, a thousand poets—
   What is one more or less?

I: Tea every evening, thousands of cups,
   Yet how fragrant. Are you not thirsty?

FULL MOON OVER THE ARCADIAN SHOPPING CENTER

Come Pan goat-god
a full moon rides
the black sky seize us
with goat-stomp goat-stink
furred shanks rank
with sweat and semen
moon-crazed Choice Pets
strain toward their master
master us too set yowling
the tame the neutered
married and middle-aged
impale The Video King
who holds in thrall
green girls and boys
with weightless eros
spooled light
shout satyr-songs crater
Volvos in your dance
warp all grids hammer
blacktop to rubble
deliver the black earth
horned god smash
The Country Wine Shoppe
hoarded sunlight the blue
grape's milk stoppered
racked in iron cradles
with split hooves kick in
the door of Mickey D's
piss in the frying vats
let tomorrow's first shift
find freezers gaping meat

crawling flesh set free
Pan we are dying
no blood of giants
no grinding our mother's bones
to loaves can sustain us
you alone Pan
be food to us be drink
possess us God of All
let the weight of your fornications
flatten all cultivars
only weeds shall thrive
jewelweed chicory loosestrife
that split the pavement to live
here is your new Arcadia
come goat-god come tonight
while the full moon rides low
and bathes The Arcadian Shopping Center
in liquid marble pulsing
like the arched torso
the bowed shuddering limbs
of your favorite boy or maiden

ASHES

There are much more likely things this box could hold—
binoculars, bridge deck and scorepads, scented soap—
than my mother in plastic: the fire's work (four years cold)
fueled by starvation, cigarettes, and dope.
Inside, instead of dowager-silver flakes,
a last edition soft as Ivory Snow,
are scoops of some beach the cold Atlantic rakes:
ground mollusk, crustacean husks, and rock that show
through the bag like gritty oatmeal.
                                                    When the great
weight of you lifted I thought, she's nothing now.
Not true. There are remains. I'm four years late
in giving these to earth, and finding how
remains beget remains. Where will you turn
up next? Always, there's something left to burn.

PART TWO

BIRDSONG,

      glaze-smooth
              reasonless
green on the skin,
         held us—

the bird itself
     lost in the full
         leaves only the bough
     just left or lighted on
        swaying

(certitude's liquid vanishing)—

in a state of
       suspended
           interpretation until abruptly
       like all oracles

              it ceased.

BUG

An apple seed, a speck on the porch rail,
he lay upturned, his six legs firing off
convulsively, six stick-figures waving,
frantic boaters stranded in a squall.

I reached to right him. What made me withdraw?
Eco-reason counseled a cool hands-off,
due deference to nature's complex synergies.
Pleased, I left him to some song-bird's craw.

But minutes later I came crawling back
and watched him weightless on my fingertip crack
blurry wings from his shell, indict my lie,
my coward's cheap *Schadenfreude*, and fly.

MIDDLE-AGED SOCKS

I have sorted the colors, whose names we seldom agree on.
I have laid one member of each pair full length against its mate.

I have rolled the back of one up the belly of the other.
I have stretched a mouth and eased both bodies inside.

Ouroboros for two, darling, and afterwards
the sweet, stupid sleep of a drawerful of kittens.

PENELOPE ASHORE

My twenty manless years
slipped like a child's fistful of sand.
The boy grew.
We lived, not meanly.
I studied cunning;
my hands wove and unwove.
When I wept a sea, they plied the oars.
Alone, I thundered through the spray
under glittering stars.

Now my husband is home
(but hardly *husband*
and not *mine*). We sleep
side by strange side:
flesh and blood
and bronze and brine.
When he straddles me
I taste the corpses and the shining ones
he murdered and embraced.

I row no longer. Where I walked
last night, a blank moon shone
white as my arms, smooth as a pebble
Pyrrha left unthrown.

MIDSUMMER POND

> . . . we row for years on the midsummer
> pond, ignorant and content.
>> Donald Hall, "Affirmation"

Walking the boat to deep water, didn't
your slimed footing betray you, and more than once?
Fronds snared your ankles and you flinched,
as if the water-snakes had marked you, flicking
prophetic tongues. In placid mid-pond,
when a deep cold rose and beat back noon
you shivered. Didn't you ever look down?
Past the oar-plashed, green-glinting surface: down,
where egg-cases, goose droppings, rope-rooted lily pads
teem and rot.

The heart's no stone, though its love song
troubles the air in widening rings. Both cease.
Snail-horn perception melts into dendrite jelly;
building pulls against the slow clasp of mud.
That is yesterday's news.
Yet this morning you found a fresh sheet of paper;
you sharpened a pencil.

HOPEFUL LIARS

Hearing the 3 a.m. freight on a bad night,
I want to hop it and chuck this mug's game.
Nailing down what's nameable is like pick-
up-sticks: reason out splinters, leave in place
a tangle of waking terrors. Careful—heaped toys
explode in agonies of writhing snakes.

My shames accuse me, poisonous as snakes;
the future's worse. Oh, for a blank midnight,
not the fladge-fiend Insomnia, who toys
with her victims in The Blaming-Maiming Game.
Stiletto-shod, she padlocks you in place
and whistles up the Tooth-Furies (who won't pick

a fight with you—they only want to pick
your bones and let them bleach). Wherever it snakes,
I'll follow the freight. Take me some other place,
take me to sleep. If that means dreams, even night-
mares, fine. Isn't every trip a carnival game
with prizes like cuddly monsters and lethal toys?

Bathed, fed, and getting cranky at their toys,
the children ride on shoulders, off to pick
a story, while the grownups play our game
of spells for space invaders, clowns, and snakes.
What hopeful liars we are, de-fanging the night:
a place for each bugbear, each bugbear in its place.

Sinking from wake to sleep, children displace
so little, their armature as light as toys.
Like animals, they're still themselves at night.

We travel deep, and it's a philosopher's pick-
le: asleep, which is the real me—the snake
or the sloughed skin—in this disappearing game?

No matter. Awake or asleep, you've got to be game;
the blue creevies will find you in either place.
I embrace all transport: train, flame, snake
or kangaroo. No, terrors aren't toys,
but raptors smell fear, and I'm a choice pick.
Better find new names for what they're after, tonight.

One last game; then the amulet-toys
are picked for bed. We play on, squatters in a place
slow night enfolds, jeweled undulant snake.

FIREWORKS OVER SING SING

C-15-94 glimpses, once a year,
the night give birth to prodigies that flare
above the guard-posts and the public shore,

arouse the unseen crowd to *ah*s, fizz out.
He despises freedom's shameless appetite
for easy rapture and release, for jets

and bombs in bloom, the splintering of jeweled
symmetry, a fury of light controlled.
They think they clap for beauty. He's not fooled:

adults or kids, they're primed down there for havoc.
He's known the bullet's sweet exploding shock
but lost his taste for mayhem, as for magic.

Why can't they learn to leave the night alone?
You wheedle from the dark what you can win.
It takes a poker face, a patient con,

and all the flash of scraping with a spoon.
The end, a light imagined like the sun,
achieved is smudgy with the discipline

of crawling there. What's free, or clear? These toys
beating the night's blue drum, the echoed applause
declare no independence, bring down no walls.

SIN-SING

By day men blasted granite, dressed and laid
the sweating 8-foot walls that shut them in.
A hard generation in a rocky place.

Galvanized buckets scrape cement towers.
Gunfire caroms off dead air,
collides with the racketing hum of a passing train.
The salt Hudson slaps empty oyster beds.

One small shift of the tongue
translates *sin* to *sing*,
but here, what music?

Men quarry more than they know.
Tonight the moon, open camellia, soaks
broad water and prison walls in copper light.

Some comfort, mother—more than day drives away.

Sing Sing Correctional Facility was named from the village in Westchester County, New York, now known as Ossining but at one time or another called Cinque Singte, Sint Sinck, or Sin-sing—all meaning "a stony place."

SOUVENIR OF SEGESTA

Crest the limestone hill
at Segesta and find the future
in ruins. Sixty talents of silver

bought this paradox under
the bright unwavering sky:
a perfect skeleton, never fleshed

and not a single column fallen.
The heart of the god never
beat here. Somewhere else

a black ram with gilded horns
screamed, blood ran
and dark wine; but nothing

stained this chalky ground.
No dwelling, no dispossession.
Sparrows have colonized

the vines hanging like hair
from the entablature; two
empty pediments stare.

What was and what will be fuse
in this palpable ghost, white
peristyle enclosing a roofless

oblong of air. Then why
do you slip that stone
in your pocket, soft shard

of the ungraspable idea?
What you really want to take home
is that small green lizard,

now motionless in the clear
noon blue, now nimbly
disappearing into the spiky

yellow-tipped brush as you
descend the shallow steps.
Lucertola, you would coax it,

green darter, until
in its flickering language
it spoke to you—

here, gone, here—
fugitive celebrant threading
the immemorial now:

stubborn dun of prickly
grasses, unconsecrated stone,
the fiery air.

According to Thucydides, the sight of this temple under construction convinced Athens to send military aid to prosperous-seeming Segesta in Sicily. But after paying 60 talents to Athens as an advance, Segesta was bankrupt, and the temple was never completed.

MORE LIGHT

To gulp down more light
the daylilies tumble
over each other, sprawling
open-mouthed toward the sun.

What cuts more, light
or longing? Their hearts
scarred a burnt-orange,
the wax petals want

nothing more. Light suffers
this radiant capture:
incandescence congealed
in a host of fallen stars.

THE GARDENER IS IN LOVE

One steals into the vernacular
sense by sense.

The wind is
a lover's thumb
that presses
and relents.

While midges raise
a local hoopla
sunset ignites
a phlox-fire of
heliotrope adoration.

Conjugate:
fold, bless, quell.

Unswerving as an oak bole
beggarly as the woolly everlasting
is desire: *verb. sap.*

THE POET AND THE HEDGEHOG

> Next morning I got up and it did not.
> Philip Larkin, "The Mower"

Call it the attraction of one prickly creature for another.
If the misanthrope poet had to prize
something in his garden,
it wouldn't be a primrose,
an oak tree,
or a songbird.
What else but a hedgehog glimpsed at dusk
in its furtive, lone routine:
an alter ego, a second genius of the place.
He "even fed it, once."

The poem he wrote after
he killed it in the blades of his mower
ends with uncharacteristic meekness
in honor—I like to think—
even love
of the mild little creature.
But maybe
what blunted the poet's barbs
and muzzled his bite was simply
the shock of ceasing,
against which (it frightened him to see)
sharpness is no defense.

SPLIT LILAC

The finches already avoid it.
    Limbs dangling, it teeters
        between elements.

What's still standing,
    root-shocked, is only
        lodged in earth,

the ruffled wing of a bird
    pitched to ground.
        Air tugs it

out of the swarming dark
    toward a dry singularity.
        Don't grieve.

Revenants need a vanishing.
    But still the violence of change
        surprises you,

though you were well schooled
    in my sudden blooms,
        my perfume.

TABERNACLES

This spreading of late summer green,
deepening almost to black, refutes
all thought of solitude.

The ear is confused by a dry swell
of vibration; unseen, the tiny faithful
offer up their racket of chitinous prayer.

Leafy rondure balks the eye,
keeps mind from measuring its single state
against the vaster curve of the horizon.

Everything is tented and tabernacled—
except those filaments catching the last
subdued light. Drifted to one side

like snow, those threads foretell the common
unraveling: a hand-clasp unlatched,
the well-knit frame thrown down, inmate dislodged.

LEAVING SODOM

They did not look back

Because the streets melted like wax
Because who would plant the turnips?
Because the angel said not to
Because the dog with the can tied to his tail died
Because they would gloat and they should pity
Because even a frog has eyes
Because stars are sown for the righteous
Because they would pity
Because justice blossoms from the bitter almond tree
Because the dead gnaw the feet of the living
Because you can't haul the moon out of a well
Because they would not understand
Because fear would be their meat and anger their pillow
Because they would understand

She looked back

Because
       in the roaring black
           flame and bituminous
   raining molten
             stone collapse of ash-
   choked night-for-day a

      sweet clear voice
       sang:

There is no river but memory
Raise up, raise up a pillar of our tears

BEETHOVEN BRIDGE

When you imagined him driving the thousand miles,
the straight highway was a razor's edge at your heart.

Like some crazy Roebling of the ether,
you conceived a span from here to there

of tensile magnetic tapes unspooling,
gorgeous and liquid: the Beethoven Bridge.

From your old LPs, scratchy with wear,
you dubbed the nine symphonies (Szell and the Cleveland),

all thirty-two piano sonatas, the late quartets
and *Fidelio*. Three days and nights

you soaked the neighborhood in a glory of sound,
so that, speeding away from you on the interstates,

he might find himself suspended above the inexorable,
and recognize, encoded among the millions of random

swimmers in our ocean of air, your love,
its pulse more rhythmic than accidents of blood,

more dependable, unending, unsinkable as music.

THREE SONGS FOR *KING LEIR*

1. Cordeilla

Where nothing grew I set a knot of herbs,
Wholesome plants—hyssop, thyme, rue.
Afternoons, he dozes in the sweet air.

Against the stone walls I espaliered roses.
I have watched the bees, flashing gold
While he sleeps, halo his white hair.

Green throat of summer, you are only a flourish
Of my sole monarch, my familiar root.
Nothing begets in me; I am nothing's heir,

Impatient to come into my kingdom. When the bees,
Blurring like smoke, sail off to hive themselves
In oak, when soil and stone are laid bare

I seat him by the fire, steady the cup
As he drinks, rub his feet. Then there are
His hair and beard to trim, his nails to pare.

In other versions of Shakespeare's play, the old king survives and his daughter, called
Cordeilla, marries Edgar.

2. Leir

Unstring the harp
Beat the hedges
Rid me of the lark
Thrush linnet
They will not
Peace at my bidding
Their music kills me
Let fall

When I would sleep
The nightingale sings
No cause, no cause
Find out who taught her
Whip him straight
She should be Gorgon-voiced
So I a man of stone
Her music kills me
Let fall

He that catches me
A pair of crickets
To scrape their legs
When I am merry
Or a leathern bat
Shall squeak me lullabye
I will thank him
For my music
Let fall

3. Edgar

Who can I tell? I miss my disguises.
Simply myself, I shall never be as wise as
Poor Tom or as strong as the Black Knight
Avenging Father's eyes, thwarting his suicide.
My clumsy self, briefly without a part,
Blurted out truth and stopped the old man's heart.

I hereby vow, for all the old men's sake,
To banish truth. Life is a dream; we wake
Only to execution. The old king
Shall not so much as stub a toe. Nothing
Arresting, unyielding, not the mildest friction
Shall touch him. Grant me, gods, the gift of fiction.

ARIEL'S LEG

Ariel is fifteen the summer
she finds a bump on her ankle.
They cut off her leg at midthigh.

Miranda is fifteen too that summer.
Sullen in her parents' orbit
she plots escape velocity.

Blue midnight on the beach in Bermuda.
Miranda kisses a prince who cries,
"My salt and slippery darter

your breasts are tipped with coral!"
Oh, brave new planet.
Back home, the bastard never calls.

In gym class, one-legged Ariel
unstraps her prosthesis
and spins it across the polished floor.

It's the phantom body that's real,
the body that remembers
swimming through small-mouthed caves

and ribs of wrecks dark with sea kelp.
The re-membered body, in spite
of saw-toothed light descending everywhere.

THE SIGHTING

I almost missed the great turtle's quiet
shimmy off the bank and into the pond:
mud, carapace, and water for an instant
three incarnations of one substance, three
siblings or three images from an alchemist's dream
    the chocolate earth
        the bottle-brown-green translucency
           the gold-flecked disc of tortoise-shell.

On stumpy flippers it ferried itself out
and stopped midway between the shores,
floating ponderously; two tiny bulges
on the leathery end of a chewed cigar were watchful.
Shocking, the improbable grace of an ugly thing.
    And then it turned
        its back on me, heaved up its rear
           and plummeted with the certainty of stone.

That day I thought the turtle was my emblem,
voyager between worlds, no more at home
in light and air than lapped like a rock by the glistening
dappled water or inching along the murk.
I longed to dive with it down to what I fear—
    mud in the nostrils
        between the clenched teeth, mud
           mud in the throat, my beginning—

to struggle back to the surface spitting out
tadpoles sweetgrass pearls prayers my mother's names.
What I need to know is in the slime
is at the bottom where the turtle goes

is in the broth it paddles in and feeds on.
    It eats and holds
        the mystery digested and dispersed:
            it is the elements it moves among.

Today I think, my angel not my emblem.
Only a god can know and be at once,
untroubled as a stone. From a life of slow
incessant journeying the turtle retrieves
nothing, knows nothing, has nothing to show
    except survival
        and that beautiful petrifaction
            token of long practice in the art of descent.

PERSUASIONS OF FALL

for Kelsey Bergstrom

It makes its own silence, an avalanche of
light that jags past the boles, pours over ochre-
tented branches, and becomes the air: fed straight
into lungs, brain, and the begging senses, till
vagrancy finds itself suddenly at home,

and poverty slinks off, inaudible now
whatever its mutterings, under all that
Gold, gold! A sliding quiet answers desire;
the heart beats to no end. But, for the fire's sake,
call it purgatory of apples, peace, home.

And not alone. A flock of migrant finches
stitches counterpoint through the trees in dark blue
chevrons, each brief flight a rising or dropping
cadence from yellow to bare brown to yellow.
A toppled tree thrusts what's left of its roots home

to the light where improbably pink mushrooms
crown the inversion. Does darkness win? No doubt
there's a strong persuasion in favor of just
that, an undersong caught in the throat of full
brilliance, something about ripeness, cold stars, home.

BETWEEN ROCKLAND AND CAMDEN

in memory of A.V.B. and M.V.B.

I drove back to forty years ago
and photographed it.
Look, the house is unchanged,
still dark-shingled, buffered by pines.
Here, still sloping away, is the sunny
garden where a child pinched snapdragons
to make them open their jaws.

Petals drop; the sexual blossom—
anthers, ovary, style—stands bare.
But function fades too, falls to junk.
Against all odds, there it still stands:
a miracle, but without the power to save.

Here is the photo I didn't take
showing a house that isn't there.
Two red-brick chimneys frame
a perfect spiral staircase
ending in mid-air. Spent fires
rise as pure beauty, keeping no one warm.

Clean as a camera's shutter-click,
sunlit rubble winks through balusters
on the unhoused stair.

Ruin's a progressive revelation.
Tomorrow or next week a crowbar
will have scavenged the polished rail,
collapsed the treads like playing cards.
Those taper chimneys, unmortared
by cold chisel and hammer, will be patching
someone's walkway or garden wall.

Memory must lie down
with rose bricks in rust-colored clay,
stiffen in change as in seawater,
sorrow fire it to ash.
Close your eyes.
First one foot, then the other. Slowly.
Those are your directions.
Fingertips graze
nothing to tell you if you're
climbing, straying, getting anywhere
so vast is the curve of this spiral stair.

NOVEMBER LIGHT

Noon

The wind attacks
a heap of brown leaves
that will not scatter. Resistance

lifts them to sunlight,
a pinwheel
the color of honey.

Four o' Clock

Light shows gracious in retreat,
thin pink horizon
below the banked cloud.

Just before shut-down
a vertical knife-edge flashes
yellow combustion.

Night

The black cyclorama, foil
to a cold white moon and one low star
huge, graspable, outlandish.

My westward drive, re-routed
only at the last moment
by the lamp-lit detour home.

THE REHEARSAL

Another evening's plain miracle.
Rose medallions stain
the river's mackerel glitter,
flushed air and water,
l'amour courtois.

But how quickly light and color
gather weight, pumping the gunmetal
hulk full of inky holes. Now
it's curtains, a last act
of insubstantiation:

sky-show extinguished
river's body dissolved
in one unimpeded
immaculate
black flood.

THE PARTY

Last night I gave a party for my dead.
They arrived together on time, even the cats.

The living room was ready—vase of gray iris,
upholstered chairs invitingly bedded in dirt—

but the guests swarmed the kitchen. I'll admit
I probably should have given more thought

to party snacks. But who the hell knows
what the dead like to eat? As it turned out

they weren't fussy. Maple syrup swigged
straight from the bottle. Raw eggs, shell and all.

Stringy meat blackening on the bone,
tomato paste furry with blue mold.

Plastic tofu, chick peas in viscous suspension
and much more, with deft fingers groping

my dead exhumed, devoured with bloodless lips.
Silent, they ate me out of house and home.

When it was all gone, they leaned exhausted
on one another, their eyes fixed on the floor.

The cats clamped teeth on tails and hurtled as one
off the top shelf, draping Aunt Birdie's neck.

Hunger will break through stone walls, she said
just before she melted across my threshold

leaving me ankle deep in empties
to shift for myself on appetite's littering tides.

THE MIDNIGHT CLEAR

Thanks to the architects of the Tower of Bauble
you can take an escalator to the moon
instead of howling at it.
Enter into their gates around Thanksgiving

and into their Food Courts with praise.
For the cities of the plain begat
suburbs, and in those precincts of pleasure
the lion and the lamb lie down,

while wolves in sheep's clothing skank it up
like there's no tomorrow.
This season irony brims the fathers' cups,
runs in the gutters like sour wine

till the children's teeth are set on edge.
A few shepherds not a-buying,
the odd prophet in love with loss
are left to heed the midnight song.

Resist all chimes. Go home
if you have one. Fall down
before your drawer full of mismatched socks.
Give thanks for your chambered heart.

NEW YEAR'S DAY

for Joe

Love, do you remember New Year's Day
racing north to beat the first snow?
Pale scraps spun and swirled on turbulent drafts
in solemn celebration of the new—
or so I half-believed, although you scoffed.

We passed three long sedans, inked Japanese
calligraphy in windows papered white,
three frames unrolling in a slow, black frieze.
Ahead, instead of thicker-gusting snow,
a battered pick-up crawled, its bed piled high
with blossoms heaped like coats on New Year's Eve.

A steady wind was stripping floral wreaths
of petals, cardboard cards, and bits of leaf,
reducing all indifferently to snow.
Above the truck, nailed to a makeshift mast,
a woman's face, enormous, sightless, mild
shuddered in the headwind. We passed

speeding under the low, quilted sky
like bride and groom escaping the wedding guests,
ducking heads and holding collars close,
impatient for the embrace of ordinariness.

Grateful acknowledgement is made to publications in which the following
poems previously appeared:

Black Dirt: "Wild Mushrooms"
California Quarterly: "Enough"
Confrontation: "Tabernacles," "The Wig"
Eclipse: "Penelope Ashore"
The Evansville Review: "Fireworks Over Sing Sing"
Global City Review: "The Sighting"
Inkwell: "Pet Fish"
Mars Hill Review: "Beethoven Bridge," "February Elegy for Al"
The Missouri Review: "Ariel's Leg," "Knives," "Leaving Sodom," "The Party,"
    "Spares," "Split Lilac"
Natural Bridge: "The Poet and the Hedgehog"
Parnassus: Poetry in Review: "Fallingwater"
Rattapallax: "The Company of Fools"
Rhino 2002: "Two Onion Études"
Smartish Pace (2002 Erskine J. Poetry Prize): "Kyushu Eclogue"
Tampa Review: "Between Rockland and Camden," "Without You"
Visions: "London Bridge"
2002 Emily Dickinson Award Anthology (University West Press): "Ariel's Leg"

Thanks also to Michael Glaser, Kate Johnson, Vickie Karp, Gerry LaFemina,
    Bern Mulvey, Grace Schulman